ONLY *the* BEST INTENTIONS

A Modern Romance Between a Guy, a Girl, and a Game

Integrated Skills Through Drama

Her Own Worst Enemy
A serious comedy about choosing a career
Alice Savage

Only the Best Intentions
A modern romance between a guy, a girl, and a game
Alice Savage

Out of Control *(Forthcoming)*
In a flood, is it better to take chances or play it safe?
Alice Savage

Teacher Resource Books

Successful Group Work —*13 Activities to Teach Teamwork Skills*
Patrice Palmer

Classroom Community Builders — *Activities for the First Day and Beyond*
Walton Burns

The Open End — *Stories for Learning, Discussion, and Expansion* *(forthcoming)*
Taylor Sapp

Keeping the Essence in Sight — *From Practice and Observation to Reflection and Back Again* *(forthcoming)*
Sharon Hartle

We are a small, independent publishing company that specializes in resources for teachers in the area of English language learning. We believe that a good teacher is resourceful, with a well-stocked toolkit full of ways to elicit, explain, guide, review, encourage, and inspire. We help stock that teacher toolkit by providing teachers with practical, useful, and creative materials.

Sign up for our mailing list on our website, www.alphabetpublishingbooks.com, for announcements about new books, and for discounts and giveaways you won't find anywhere else.

ONLY *the* BEST INTENTIONS

A Modern Romance Between a Guy, a Girl, and a Game

ALICE SAVAGE

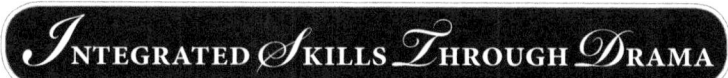

Copyright 2018 by Alice Savage

ISBN: 978-1-948492-06-5 (paperback)
978-1-948492-07-2 (epub)
978-1-948492-10-2 (kindle)

Library of Congress Control Number: 2017964682

All rights reserved. No part of this book may be reproduced, introduced into or stored in a retrieval system, or transmitted, in any form, or by any means (electronic, mechanical, photocopying, recording, or otherwise) without the prior written permission of the copyright holder.

Country of Manufacture Specified on the Last Page

First Printing 2018

Published by: Alphabet Publishing, 1204 Main Street #172, Branford, Connecticut 06405 USA

info@alphabetpublishingbooks.com • www.alphabetpublishingbooks.com

Designed by James Arneson Art & Design, JaadBookDesign.com

All interior artwork licensed from Adobestock or Depositphotos, except as acknowledged below:
GeForce GTX AllStar Tournament, page 19 Alper Çuğun (cc-by 2.0 license);
3rd Place Match SLTV StarSeries Summer Split, page 20, Yuri Shornikov (cc-by 2.0 license),

The author consulted a number of sources while researching the articles and we would like to acknowledge them below: "Life in the Age of Screens"—*Alone Together: Why We Expect More from Technology and Less from Each Other* by Sherry Turkle; "Connected, but alone?", a TED Talk by Sherry Turkle; "In Constant Digital Contact, We Feel 'Alone Together'" *Fresh Air* Oct. 17 2012 (https://www.npr.org/2012/10/18/163098594/in-constant-digital-contact-we-feel-alone-together); *Irresistible: The Rise of Additive Technology and the Business of Keeping Us Hooked* Adam Alter; *Proteus paradox: How Online Games and Virtual Worlds Change Us—and How They Don't* by Nick Yee; "'Our minds can be hijacked': the tech insiders who fear a smartphone dystopia" by Paul Lewis. *The Guardian*, Oct. 5 2017.

"A Gamer in the Family"—"The Overwatch Videogame League Aims to Become the New NFL" by Nathan Hall. WIRED, Dec. 5 2017. (https://www.wired.com/story/overwatch-videogame-league-aims-to-become-new-nfl/); "Geguri to become first female competitor in Overwatch APEX" by Young Jae Jeon. ESPN.com, Aug. 7 2017 (http://www.espn.com/esports/story/_/id/20269551/geguri-become-first-female-competitor-overwatch-apex); "Faker apparently has a monthly allowance of $178" by Andrew Kim. Slingshot, October 26, 2017 (http://slingshotesports.com/2017/10/26/faker-parents-allowance/); "Faker: 'Now I do want to go on a date… If I ever have time, I will consider meeting someone.'" LOL Matrix, July 9, 2017. (http://lol.esportsmatrix.com/en-US/News/Detail?id=4853); "Do You Have 'Gaming Disorder,' A Newly Recognized Mental Health Condition?" by Bruce Lee. Forbes, Dec. 24 2017 (https://www.forbes.com/sites/brucelee/2017/12/24/do-you-have-video-gaming-disorder-a-newly-recognized-mental-health-condition/); "Stefano "Verbo" Disalvo: Defining the Los Angeles Valiant Brotherhood" Overwatch League. Nov. 21 2017. (https://valiant.overwatchleague.com/news/stefano-verbo-disalvo-defining-los-angeles-valiant-brotherhood); Gamepedia s.v. "Faker" (https://lol.gamepedia.com/Faker); "The Rise of a Legend—The Story of Lee "Faker" Sang-hyeok" by Zir0. Dot Esports. Apr. 8 2015 (https://dotesports.com/league-of-legends/news/the-rise-of-a-legend-the-story-of-lee-faker-sanghyeok-7218) ; "Gaming and Gamers" by Maeve Duggan. Pew Research Center, Dec. 15 2015 (http://www.pewinternet.org/2015/12/15/gaming-and-gamers/); and interviews with the author.

"The Rise of Esports"—"The Sports Market" AT Kearney (https://www.atkearney.com/documents/ 10192/6f46b880-f8d1-4909-9960-cc605bb1ff34); "Esports revenues will reach $696M in 2017 and $1.5Bn by 2020" by Peter Warman. Newzoo, Feb. 14 2017 (https://newzoo.com/insights/articles /esports-revenues-will-reach-696-million-in-2017/); "Dota 2's $20 Million International Starts Today" by Brain Albert. IGN.com, Aug. 3 2016 (http://www.ign.com/articles/2016/08/03/dota-2s-20-million-international-starts-today).

Thank you to my family for loving theatre, especially Cyrus and Kaveh Shafiei because you remind me how much I love it, too. Also, Jorj for keeping on keeping on.

I also want to thank Carnegie Theatre's Steward Savage for his insight into the value of background research and the acting students for helping to workshop the script through readings and recordings. Cyrus, Jackson, Kaveh, Sadie, and Viviana thank you! Also, Davis and Sam, you showed up and worked hard!

I am also extremely grateful to my colleagues at Lone Star College for believing in me, and for working with me on developing the material. Thanks Amy, Anne, Colin, David, Erin, Janet, Joy, Katie, Macarena, and Masoud. You are all gifted teachers, and I love working with you!

Finally, I want to thank Ken Wilson for your wise counsel and Walton Burns for taking a chance on an unconventional manuscript. It has been a pleasure!

—A.S.

Contents

INTRODUCTION   *1*
   How to Use This Book   *3*

PREVIEW   *7*
   Think about the Topic   *7*
   Discuss the Title   *7*
   Read for Background   *9*
      ▸ *Life in the Age of Screens*   *10*
      ▸ *A Gamer in the Family*   *14*
      ▸ *The Rise of Esports*   *19*
   Practice Attentive Listening   *23*

ONLY THE BEST INTENTIONS   *25*
   Read the Script   *25*
   Discussion   *47*

PRODUCTION   *49*
   Analyze the Play   *49*
   Assign Roles   *50*
   Learn Your Part   *50*
   Rehearse   *53*
   Practice Pronunciation   *54*
      ▸ *Sentence Stress to Clarify and Show Contrast*   *55*
      ▸ *Pronunciation and linking*   *55*
   Stage Your Play   *56*

POST-PERFORMANCE   *59*
   Lead a Talkback   *59*
   Write an Alternative Ending   *59*
   Gather Language   *60*

Have a Mini-Debate	60
Create a Sequel	60
Practice Pragmatics: Managing interpersonal conflict	61
ASSESSMENT	**65**
Teacher Evaluation Rubric	66
Peer Feedback Questions	67
Self-Reflection Questions	68
BEYOND THE CLASSROOM	**69**
Publish an Interview About Screen Time	69
SAMPLE PERFORMANCE DAILY SCHEDULE	**71**
ABOUT THE AUTHOR	**73**

Introduction

THE LANGUAGE CLASSROOM is a great place for drama. When you produce a play, you combine both language and skills practice. You study vocabulary, grammar, and pronunciation. You also study conversations and develop strategies for interacting with others. Plays can demonstrate the phrases and expressions we use when we make friends, express frustration, praise talent, and reach other conversational goals.

In this book, you will have a chance to work on all these skills by preparing and performing a play. Through background readings and discussions, you will develop your vocabulary and explore the themes of the play. Through focused stress, intonation, and pronunciation work, you will learn to communicate the emotional intentions of your message, as well as learn the sounds of words in connected speech. Finally, through the production of a play, you will explore culture and expressive

language while performing the sometimes serious, sometimes funny, struggles of a serious computer gamer, his fiancée, and the lively family he hopes to marry into.

A special feature of this book is the opportunity to work on something called **pragmatics**. Pragmatics describes the skill of getting messages across through the culturally appropriate use of language and gesture. Everyone uses pragmatics in their own language, but it is practiced in different ways among different communities. When people are good at the pragmatics of a language, they reach their goals without hurting their relationships.

Here is an example:

Mike lives alone. He would like an invitation to a holiday dinner from his friend Lin. Mike says to Lin, "What are you doing for Thanksgiving?" Lin explains that she and her husband are having a few relatives over. "Oh, that sounds nice," says Mike. There is a pause. Lin says, "What are you doing for the holiday?" and Mike says, "Oh, nothing." There is another pause. Lin says, "Well, why don't come to our house? It's a simple gathering, but we'd love to have you." Mike is happy. "Oh, great!" he says, "Thank you so much. That's very kind of you!" and the conversation continues.

In this short exchange, Mike communicates his desire for an invitation indirectly. Mike cannot say, "Can I come to your house for Thanksgiving?" because that would not be polite. He would be putting Lin in an awkward position because it would be hard for her to say no. Instead, Mike creates the conditions for Lin to understand his situation. Then *she* can decide to invite him or not without feeling uncomfortable or rude.

In this instance, Mike is demonstrating good social skills, which is another way of saying he's good at pragmatics. However, this is only true if Lin is happy with the conversation as well. If Lin feels that Mike has pushed her to make the offer, she will use her own pragmatics skills to let him know that his efforts to get an invitation were inappropriate.

Pragmatics skills are most useful in challenging situations. These situations rarely appear in textbooks, which is why pragmatics is often considered a hidden language. In fact, people tend to need pragmatics most during uncomfortable or important conversations. In these cases, people with good pragmatics skills use special phrases to signal their intention. For example, look at the sentence, "I don't want you to take this the wrong way, but I don't think singing is for you."

The expression *I don't want you to take this wrong way, but . . .* is a familiar signal in English. It is how you can warn someone that you are about to say something that is truthful, but not complimentary. When the listener knows criticism is coming, they can prepare for it. There are many of these signal phrases that you can use to feel in control of a conversation. A play is a good place to learn them because you can experience the expressions in a social and emotional context.

In addition to pragmatics, you will have opportunities to practice the more familiar skills of pronunciation. You can develop a natural tone, effective intonation, and even use gestures because you will be speaking high frequency phrases in contexts typically used by family members and friends. You may notice that your voice goes up or down, or slower or faster, depending on the mood of your character. Sometimes you will try to speak in a joking way. At other times, you will show frustration or confusion.

Word and sentence stress will also be important. As you rehearse, you must make decisions about which content words to emphasize to best support your meaning. You'll say these words louder and clearer so the audience will understand. You'll also become aware of syllable stress in longer words. Having the right stress helps people recognize the word when you are saying it.

Finally, you'll have a chance to practice free conversation skills when you read and discuss the topics in the background articles and prepare to perform the play. You'll share opinions, give reasons, make suggestions, offer and respond to advice, and provide encouragement to your peers. These are all useful academic and workplace abilities.

After the play, you will find additional activities for repurposing the content and language in new ways. Hopefully, by the end of this book, you'll feel a little more confident about your English conversational skills, especially when talking about the role of technology, the Internet, and esports, and how these new media are impacting human relationships. If that is not preparing for the future, what is?

HOW TO USE THIS BOOK

The activities and ideas in this book are presented in a specific sequence. However, the book is designed to be flexible. You can use it alone or to support another book. Some teachers may take a full session to work on the play and the accompanying activities. A longer time frame allows you to use some of the post-performance activities to go deeper into research and skills development throughout the rehearsal period. Other teachers might want to work on the play one day each week to prepare for a final end-of-session performance. Still others may take a week, skip over some of the activities, shorten rehearsal time, and have students read with a script in hand. However you decide to do it, students working in collaboration will benefit from their experience with conversational English.

The best way to plan your theatre production is to read through the background readings, script, and post-performance activities. Then decide on an approach that best fits your students' level, your curricular objectives, and your schedule. Also decide how much you will need to be involved in supporting the production. For many classes, the students are able to do much of the work themselves.

You can mix and match the activities to fit your curricular objectives. There are texts that can be expanded to work on reading skills. There are discussion and writing prompts that allow students to analyze the topic from different perspectives. These can also be used as preparation for a mini-debate on the role of screens in family life—a major theme of *Only the Best Intentions*.

To plan the production, think carefully about your schedule. You want students to feel a sense of accomplishment at the end. Having students memorize lines, block, rehearse, and perform a play is rewarding but it takes an investment of time and energy. If you don't have the time, you can aim for a rehearsed reading in the style of Reader's Theater and still reap many of the benefits (For Reader's Theatre support go to http://www.alphabetpublishingbooks.com/integrated-skills-through-drama).

There are a number of ways to adjust the materials to the level of your class. This module is designed for intermediate levels and up. For lower levels, you could simply use the play as a text. You can do the activities and discuss the characters' decisions and the plot, as well as the topic of choosing a college major. Then you can have students practice reading the parts from the script to work on sounds and intonation. For middle levels, you might have students memorize and perform the play, but do a rehearsed or staged reading (see page 49 for some ideas on how to produce the play). To increase the challenge for higher levels, do a full performance. Have students memorize lines and perform for another group, or even create a video to be shown to a wider audience. Also, feel free to allow students to adapt the script to suit their goals.

If you have several groups stage the same play, consider small changes such as having a male actor play the lead, or having some of the groups rewrite a specific scene, such as the ending, or even write new scenes (Feel free to change names in the script to reflect different genders or countries as needed). Small adaptations like this will allow you and the students to be creative while keeping the show fresh from one performance to the next. If groups produce different plays, you may want to start performances with a short introduction to the script's central issues. This can be done by the director as a way to help the audience follow the plot. In addition, you can also add or double up roles. However, it is a good idea to have at least one person who does not act and can take on the role of director, videographer, and/or stage manager. For more ideas see the suggestions below.

While students are rehearsing, you can circulate, take notes, and provide language and skills support as needed. You can also meet with each group to give specific feedback on pronunciation or scene work. Some groups may need more encouragement than others, but as long as the play is comprehensible, and they have the language skills to communicate with each other, they should be able to produce a play with minimal support.

You also have choices on how you handle performances. Some teachers like to do all the plays on the same day, while others do one a day for two or more days. If your class is doing one play, you might perform for a different class, perhaps one at a lower level. In any case, allow 25 to 30 minutes for each performance, and consider doing a talkback or having classmates give feedback at the end. (See the post-performance section on page 59)

Finally, there are ideas for different types of assessment at the end of the book. If using a rubric such as the one on page 66, it is a good idea to give it to the students at the beginning of the production so they know what you will value.

Most importantly, enjoy the process! Experiment. Think critically. Be creative. And above all, have fun!

Suggestions for different class sizes

Different classes have different numbers of students. This can present a challenge when producing a play, so here are some suggestions for making sure all students are engaged. By dividing the class into groups and giving each group a project, you can provide practice for everyone. One way to do this is to give students a preference sheet. Some may prefer to act. Others may prefer to participate in a debate.

Group one: Produce the play as is.

Group option two: Produce one of the other plays in Alphabet Publishing's Integrated Skills through Drama series. Have the two groups perform for each other.

Group option three: Organize and have a debate based on the readings and possibly some outside research on the topic. See page 60. And see the materials for structuring a mini-debate on the Alphabet website at: http://www.alphabetpublishingbooks.com/integrated-skills-through-drama.

Group option four: Have one or two videographers make a documentary about the process. They can interview and film the actors as they prepare for their roles. Then the videographers can edit the video and share it with the class.

Group option five: Write and produce a short sequel to the play. Create enough characters so that everyone has a role. See page 60 for ideas.

Group option six: Use the Pragmatics Lesson on page 61 to create a short play.

Preview

Look at the photos and discuss your answers to the questions below:

THINK ABOUT THE TOPIC

a. How would you describe the personal lives of the people in these pictures?
b. How are computer gamers similar to athletes? How are they different?
c. Do you agree with this statement: "When people are in love, they will not let anyone or anything get in their way?"

DISCUSS THE TITLE

Read the examples with the phrase *best intentions* below. What do you think happened in each situation? What does *best intentions* mean in each case?

a. **One roommate to another:** Oh no! Now you are really sick. I'm so sorry I made you eat those eggs. I had the best intentions. I thought eating something would make you feel better.

_____

_____

b. **A teacher to a student:** Joe meant well, but sometimes the best intentions don't work out the way you hope. Next time, he offers to help you with your homework, just politely say no.

c. **A mother to a four-year-old daughter:** I know you had the best intentions, honey, but your little brother did not really need a haircut.

Best intentions

In English, we often use the phrase *He (or She) had only the best intentions* after someone has done something they thought would improve a situation, but in reality, it got worse. Even though they tried to help, things did not go the way they hoped.

We might also say it when rejecting advice. We could say, "I know you have only the best intentions, but I have specific reasons for doing it my way."

READ FOR BACKGROUND

This play explores the relationship between a computer gamer and non-gamers. To understand their struggle, it is helpful to do some background reading on the issues.

Vocabulary

Match the phrases from the texts to their meanings. Look up words or expressions that you want to learn more about. Try to use them in new sentences or dialogues.

1. _k_	have problems later even though things are okay now	a. cause for alarm
2.	a reason why people might be in danger	b. virtual worlds
3.	caused big changes in family life	c. mainstream culture
4.	feeling close to someone else by sharing feelings	d. an emotional connection
5.	online locations, often in a computer game, with maps and characters	e. a confidence boost
6.	something that happens or people do again and again in different places around the world	f. disrupted families
7.	spend time with friends online	g. a conscious effort
8.	the way most people think	h. virtually hang out with friends
9.	it is impossible for me to stop myself	i. meet expectations
10.	to behave in the way others want you to behave	j. I can't help it!
11.	something that makes you feel good about yourself	k. ~~run into trouble down the road~~
12.	a decision to do something rather than let it happen naturally.	l. a global phenomenon

READ the article about the effects of technology on modern families. Highlight and take notes on important points. Then do the discussion task after the text.

Life in the Age of Screens

In the early 2000s, sociologists became interested in the role of technology in people's lives. Social media, smartphones, and online games were entering mainstream culture, and these exciting new forms of entertainment dramatically changed how people spent time. People started having fewer face-to-face conversations and more interaction through screens. Was this a good thing or a cause for alarm?

Many researchers set out to answer this basic question. They did field work, took surveys, and observed interactions in schools, at home, and in public places. Their work is ongoing, but already there are some very interesting theories about humans and their screens. It turns out that humans are attracted to the sense of control that technology can provide. But at what cost?

Why we text

One of these researchers is Sherry Turkle. The MIT sociologist turned her investigations into a book called *Alone Together*. In her book and public talks, she explains why people started choosing texting over phone calls. According to Turkle, texting allows people to control the conversation. They can revise and edit what they say. They can also choose when to communicate and how much time they want to spend. When they are done communicating, they can just stop answering a text. They also do not have to listen to any boring or uncomfortable parts  of a conversation. In a 2012 TED Talk, she described a 15-year-old boy who said, "Someday, I'd like to learn to have a conversation, but not now." For this teenager and many other subjects, texting removed much of the emotion from the interaction and was therefore easier to handle than a real conversation.

In a different example, Turkle emphasized the potential downside of texting. In an NPR interview with Terry Gross, she talked about a young man who wanted to cancel a dinner with his grandparents. When his mother told him to call them, he heard the emotion in their voices. He sensed their excitement about spending time with him. The phone call created an emotional connection, and he changed his mind. He promised to visit them. Turkle explains this might not have happened if he had just texted that he couldn't make it.

How avatars change us

Like texting, avatars also give people a sense of control. Avatars are the characters and creatures that people become in a game or a computer simulation. Sometimes, people choose an avatar. Other  times, people can create the avatars by choosing hair color, body type, and other features. Avatars appeal to both males and females because they offer an alternative identity. While this is a little bit like getting up in the morning and choosing what clothes to wear, it can take the creation of a separate self a step further.

Nick Yee is particularly interested in avatars. The Stanford-trained researcher has done experiments that show an interesting effect of virtual reality. When people become an avatar, the physical appearance of that avatar can affect their behavior. In one of Yee's experiments, people were given an ugly or an attractive avatar. They could see their avatar in a virtual mirror, so they knew what their avatar looked like. Next, they interacted with another avatar. The people with good-looking avatars were more confident and shared more. The people with the ugly avatars were less confident. The results suggest that the confidence boost of a tall, attractive avatar can make virtual worlds more appealing than real life.

The attraction of robot friends

People can also avoid messy human connections by turning to robots. Many companies now offer social robots that can serve as the "perfect" companion. The robot might be a voice in a phone or a device such as Alexa or Echo. It could also appear in a plastic human-like body or look like a soft furry animal.

Turkle sees something strange about this increase in electronic companionship. To her, it means that people are looking for the comfort of a friendship without the demands of a relationship. They hope technology will provide the perfect solution: a friend that is always available, always easy, and never needs anything in return.

Turkle finds this trend disturbing because it can lead to a culture where people do not depend on other people. They might care less about others as a result. A robot friend might make life easier, but it also might make life less meaningful. People will not have the joy of being needed. They might ask for and give fewer favors, and their friends and family members will have fewer opportunities to show their loyalty and love.

Concerns about Digital Addiction

While technology may give a sense of control, many researchers believe people need to be aware of its potential negative effects. Adam Alter is a social psychologist who argues that we should not think of addiction as just chemical. We should also think about it as behavioral. In his book, *Irresistible: The Rise of Additive Technology and the Business of Keeping Us Hooked*, Alter explains that digital addictions can affect the brain in the same way as drug addictions. Alter is concerned that millions of people around the world, especially children, are at risk. Fortunately, some countries are passing laws designed to protect society from the harmful effects of screens.

In 2018, the World Health Organization (WHO) recognized gaming addiction as a mental health disorder. This does not mean that all gamers are mentally ill, but it does show that online gaming can become a problem. The WHO describes the condition as "significant impairment in personal, family, social, educational, occupational, or other important areas of functioning." In other words, when gaming has a negative effect on a person's real life, that person may have a disorder that needs treatment.

Even industry professionals are concerned about screen time. Justin Rosenstein is one of them. In an interview with the *Guardian*, he admitted to putting parental controls on his own phone because he wanted to stop himself from downloading apps. Rosenstein is an interesting example because he invented the *like* button on Facebook. Now he feels regret. He believes the *like* feature is addictive and he worries about the fact that the average user now touches their phone more than two thousand times a day. He says the compulsion to go online and stay online is just as the designers intended.

In the end, most experts agree that people need to find a balance. Turkle is a consultant to technology companies, and Rosenstein continues to work with computers. Like most experts, they understand that devices are necessary and useful tools of the modern world. However, conversation and human connection are also important in the 21st century. People may simply need to make a conscious effort to include it in their lives.

Discussion

Work in groups of three. Read and discuss the questions for five minutes. Then complete one or more of the sentences below to share with the class.

1. How do you like to communicate with other people? Do you choose different media depending on the situation?
2. Do you agree that technology gives you a sense of control over conversations? Can you think of examples?
3. Do you seek out face-to-face conversations or do you avoid them? Why?

Insight sentences

1. This reading and discussion made me think more about _____
   _____

2. I realize that _____
   _____

3. For me, the hardest thing about a face-to-face conversation is _____
   _____

READ the article about the way computers can create conflict between generations. Highlight and take notes on important points. Then do the discussion task after the text.

A Gamer in the Family

In the home of an online gamer, dinner time can be a source of stress. The food is on the table, the family is waiting, and the 13-year-old is deeply involved in battling a dragon or taking a tower. Someone calls him—90% of multiplayer online battle games are played by males—and he responds, "Just a minute!" However, the minute passes, and still he does not show up. If he leaves the battle arena, he's letting his teammates down. He can't do that, so he makes his family wait.

The struggle in this household is not unique. Around the world, families must cope with the fact that many young men and women are living in two worlds. They have the reality of school, family responsibilities, and other activities. Then they have the virtual reality of a game in which they build an identity, a skill set, and a social life that may feel as important to them as the people in their real world.

Parental expectations

Many parents see gaming as a threat. When mothers and fathers see their child in a dark room, lit only by a screen with flashing explosions, they feel alarm. And when that kid makes a choice not to come to the table because he has to finish a game, they are hurt. The average parent today did not grow up playing multiplayer online games such as League of Legends, StarCraft, or World of Warcraft, so their idea of a normal childhood is different from their children's. For the older generation, childhood means going outside, playing in the park, meeting friends, learning to climb trees, ride a bike, or one of many other activities that involve a physical rather than a virtual experience.

This conflict between parental ideas and children's preferences often grows worse during the early teenage years. Parents can use parental controls with younger children, but they often expect their thirteen- and fourteen-year-olds to take on more responsibilities for organizing their time and setting goals. Many hope their child will make good choices and are disappointed when those choices do not meet their expectations (A 2015 Pew research survey reported that about a quarter of adults feel that most gaming is a "waste of time").

For gamers, negative parental attitudes can be painful, especially for players who feel passionately about their game. They may struggle to explain the rules and goals to an indifferent listener. Or a player might have an exciting win, but no one in the family cares. As a result, gamers can feel lonely.

Educational choices

A major source of conflict concerns ambition. Most parents want their children to be successful. Their children generally agree with this goal, but they may not agree on the path. For the older generation, getting good grades in school and going to college leads to a job. However, for some young people, a career in gaming is a way to make money and have fun, sometimes without going to college.

Stefano Disalvo experienced this kind of conflict with his parents. Disalvo is a Canadian gamer from Toronto, Canada. While he was growing up, he and his parents argued about his time on screen. Disalvo wanted to develop his skills and become a top player in a game called Overwatch. He began spending six hours a day practicing the game. When his mother worried that he was not paying attention to his schoolwork, she limited his time. Then she took away his modem.

Disalvo persisted. In an interview with *WIRED*, he explains how he got around his parents' rules. Even though he could not play, he made his own maps of the game and worked on techniques. He also tried out for teams in California. Then one day he sat down and told his parents he was not going to college. He had a contract with a professional Overwatch team called the Immortals. Sponsored by the gaming company, the team would pay him a salary and provide free housing, even a 401(k) plan. Disalvo wanted to move to California to train for competition at the highest level. His parents realized that he had a career opportunity, and they accepted his decision.

Disalvo says that now he and his parents have a better relationship. His career has continued to grow, so his story has a positive outcome. However, there are thousands of young men with a similar desire, and they will never become pro gamers. Those that do can expect a short career of five or six years before their skills begin to decline. At that point, they might move into coaching, casting, or another game-related job, but those jobs are not guaranteed. Many ambitious gamers can still become jobless in their 20s.

A number of Disalvo's teammates are Korean, where traditional family life is highly respected, so conflicts with parents can be painful. Korea produces many of the world's top gamers, and Korean families face the same educational dilemmas as Americans. In Seoul and other cities, ambitious gamers go to special cafes called PC bangs. PC bangs are open twenty-four hours so players can practice. The hours spent at these cafes are hours not spent at home with family or studying. Instead, players are working on skills and strategies. Many of them hope to find a sponsor or coach so they can become professionals. Their

parents may be aware of the potential of esports, but they still worry. Should they support a career in gaming or guide their child to attend college and work toward a traditional profession?

Kim Se-hyeon is one of these children. Se-hyeon started playing computer at the age of 5, and when she discovered the game Overwatch, she loved it. She went to PC bangs and became a competitive player. Playing as Geguri, which means *frog* in Korean, she joined an all-female team and became famous for her skill. In fact, she was so good that other players thought she was cheating.

Se-hyeon's parents worried about her, and when her friend was injured and left the team, they brought their daughter back home to complete her education. For Se-hyeon, it was a difficult time. She had no interests outside of Overwatch and all her friends were players. Eventually her parents allowed her to go to a school that gave her a flexible schedule. They accepted her passion for gaming, and she is now on a new team.

In recent years, educational institutions have become more accepting of esports, and a few colleges and universities are starting leagues and offering scholarships for top gamers. This means, a dedicated player can continue to play while studying for a more traditional degree. However, only a small number of schools provide this opportunity.

Dating and marriage

Most professional gamers sacrifice relationships to focus on their sport. One of the top Korean gamers, Lee Sang-hyeok, recently told reporters that he might start thinking about a relationship if he ever has time. The League of Legends champion who has the game name Faker has simply been too busy up to now. Faker is not alone. Many gamers are single or marry other gamers.

However, most adult players are not professionals. They have jobs, spouses, and often children. A married person has little free time, and couples often have conflicts when one spouse plays but the other does not. Social science researcher and cofounder of Quantic Foundry, Nick Yee, explains that if people play together, the relationship can work, but when one partner plays a game alone, it can cause stress in a marriage. The spouses of gamers often complain about the time taken from the family by the game.

This is a challenge for Rachel and Jack Greaves. The couple live in Norfolk, Virginia where Jack has a job with the U.S. Navy. Because he is often on a ship for weeks at a time, he plays a lot of computer games for entertainment. When he comes back, he says he has problems adjusting. In fact, he may be slightly addicted to the game, StarCraft II.

"He gets up at four am to play computer games because he knows I'll get angry if I catch him," says Rachel. The couple have twins, two four-year-old boys, and she worries that Jack is setting a bad example.

Jack says he has a stressful life, and playing helps him relax and be a better husband and father. After much discussion, the couple has agreed on a schedule. Jack gives the boys a bath, reads them a story, and puts them to bed. After they go to sleep, he can play for an hour. Sometimes he still gets up early for a quick game before work, but he tries to hide it from Rachel. This is not an ideal situation, but it is a common one.

Yee points out that games are designed to be appealing. People want to feel valuable, and the game makes players feel needed. When Jack defends his StarCraft team and saves a virtual life, he gets a sense of satisfaction and a confidence boost. He also enjoys playing with his two boys in the real world, but it is sometimes difficult to find a balance. "I know gaming is a time suck," he says, "but I can't help it. I like it!"

In contrast to the Greaves, Rob Salisbury and his wife Beth are both occasional gamers, and they frequently play together. In fact, the parents often play games against their two sons, and win. The Salisburys are educators, and understand the importance of real world experience, so they limit screen time, but gaming is source of family fun rather than conflict.

Gaming is not the only way that screens have changed family life, but the attraction of modern computer games has disrupted many families. Perhaps couples need to have a deep conversation about technology before they get married. They may have the best intentions when they fall in love, but unless they talk about their relationship with screens and gaming, they may run into trouble down the road.

Discussion

Work in groups of three. Read and discuss the questions for five minutes. Then complete one or more of the sentences below to share with the class.

1. How does gaming affect your family? Do you play computer games? Do your friends or family members play? Do you like to watch people play?

2. According to the article, what are the causes of conflict between parents and children over gaming? Why do they happen? How could they be handled?
3. The article suggests that gamers shouldn't marry non-gamers? Do you agree?

Insight sentences

1. This text/conversation made me think more about _____
   _____

2. I realize that _____
   _____

3. I think family members of a computer gamer should _____
   _____

READ the article about how gaming is changing sports entertainment. Highlight and take notes on important points. Then do the discussion task below.

The Rise of Esports

World Cup soccer is a big deal. During the final matches, streets are empty in cities across the world. That is because more than a billion people may be watching. And soccer is just one sport. Altogether, professional sports feed a $500 billion a year industry and their influence is expected to grow. Money is made through ticket sales, media broadcasts, advertising, sponsorships, and merchandise. Fans love their teams and are willing to pay to see them play, wear their shirts, and otherwise join in the fun of competition.

This public culture of celebrating traditional sports has been with us a long time, but another sports culture has been growing out of sight. To an outsider, this new sport does not look like a sport at all. The "athletes" sit in comfortable chairs and appear to do little more than move a mouse or type on a keyboard. Yet these players also fill sports stadiums around the world. It is not what the players are doing in the physical world that excites their fans, it is what is happening on a virtual one.

Can magical creatures battling in an artificial landscape really be called a sport Apparently, the answer is yes. Electronic sports, or esports, involve any sort of game played on a screen, and they are now a major global phenomenon just like traditional sports. In fact, according to the market research company Newzoo, the global esports economy is already around $100 billion. That is a lot of money for such a young industry.

The most publicly celebrated esports are MMOs. MMO, or sometimes MMOG, is short for Massively Multiplayer Online Game. An MMO allows human teams to take on roles and compete against other human teams. These games are similar to traditional field sports because they involve personalities working together on offensive and defensive strategies. Because humans are facing each other in competition, the variables of skill, personality, relationships, and creativity all become part of the game. Fans can get to know individual players, follow their career, and watch them struggle to get along with teammates and overcome pride, failure, and other challenges just as they would with tennis stars or celebrity basketball players.

The first modern MMOs came out around 2002 at a time when the Internet was becoming accessible to millions of new users. Before then, software controlled the gaming experience. Then Blizzard Entertainment started producing games that allowed players to make changes the map (The map is the environment where the game takes place). A player named Eul adapted a map from World of Warcraft to produce a new game. Eul called his new game DOTA (Defense of the Ancients). Then, Eul created a sequel called DOTA 2 and changed gaming forever.

In DOTA 2, there were two five-player teams of heroes. Players could collaborate with teammates to compete against another human team. This was a huge departure from games where players competed against machines. Because each hero had unique abilities and was controlled by a person, DOTA 2 was as complex and unpredictable as basketball or soccer, and it immediately became popular. People liked playing it, and they even liked to watch it. Fans began going on a website called Twitch to watch games. This increase in viewers gave game makers an opportunity to create leagues and competitions.

Now DOTA 2 tournaments, which are held in Seattle, Washington, easily fill the Key Arena, a professional sports stadium. Viewers buy tickets to sit in the seats normally used by concertgoers or basketball fans. They can see the players in clear sound-proof boxes on the floor, but the main action takes place on giant screens. People watch their favorite teams' heroes battle on the map. They cheer and boo from their seats even though the players cannot hear them. The total prize money for this tournament is over $20 million, the largest in esport history, and most of the money comes from players who pay for passes to participate in special features of the game.

DOTA may be one of the oldest games, but the most popular MMO is League of Legends. League of Legends (LOL) is a free game played around the world. More than 1 million people play each day and more than 30 million people are signed up according the game's maker, Riot Games. LOL also has world finals that take place in different countries, and they are watched by more people than baseball's world series.

Recently, a newer game called Overwatch has been getting attention. Its parent company, Blizzard, is organizing a league that is similar to professional sports. The league hires players and moves them into training houses. The players live together and work with a coach to develop strategies and skills. In addition to a salary, they can make money through sponsorships and by livestreaming their games on Twitch.

In the top levels of MMO competition, a team may be international. Korea has a strong presence in the field along with China, Japan, and the U.S. This means players may have language and cultural barriers, but they often receive support from the organization. Living together means they eat and socialize with each other. Along the way, they learn a few words of one another's languages. Over time they become skilled at communicating important information during a game.

While many countries are represented in the highest level of competitive esports, there are very few females. According to the analytics organization Quantic Foundry between 10% and 36% of MMO gamers are female, and there are no women on the top performing teams.

The gaming industry is trying to encourage more women to participate. There are now female commentators and designers as well as featured players. However, most females prefer different kinds of games. They tend to play on phones, and they prefer puzzles and simulations in which they act out stories. This is a different experience from the battle ground arenas of tournament esports that men prefer.

It is hard to predict the effect of esports on society. Research by Newzoo suggests that time spent playing and viewing online games is going up. This means the market for more traditional forms of entertainment is becoming smaller. While MMOs are not the only online games attracting public attention, they are the most public and are therefore on track to be a major force in entertainment sports in the future.

Discussion

Work in groups of three. Read and discuss the questions for five minutes. Then complete one or more of the sentences below to share with the class.

1. Do you agree that esports are a sport? Explain.
2. In your opinion, what makes esports so popular?
3. Would you consider a career in esports?

Insight sentences

1. This conversation made me think more about _____
   _____

2. I realize that _____
   _____

3. I think esports are changing entertainment sports because_____
   _____

Attentive listening

Collaborating with others requires good listening skills. When people have your attention, they can talk through their ideas. When you have their attention, you can talk through yours. Then you can work together to put the best ideas into action. Good listeners remember the ideas they hear. Then they respond to those ideas before they transition to their own ideas.

Use one of the stems below to rephrase the speaker's ideas.

- I am interested in what you said about . . .
- So you get a lot out of . . .
- So here's what I think you are saying . . .
- You make a good point about . . .

To transition, use one of the stems below to add or comment.

- So my experience is a little different . . .
- But don't you ever feel that . . .
- Yeah, you're exactly right, and I also think . . .
- What you said about . . . makes me think about. . .

PRACTICE ATTENTIVE LISTENING

Choose an appealing online site or app such as a game, an online store, a social media site, or a video channel. Then form groups of four or five for the speaking task. Use the sentence stems from the box above, or your own ideas.

a. Choose a timekeeper. The timekeeper sets a phone timer for three or four minutes and monitors the speakers to make sure they listen attentively.
b. One speaker begins by introducing his or her online activity and explaining why it's appealing.
c. Other partners respond, but each member must summarize what one previous speaker has said before continuing the conversation.
d. The time keeper stops if anyone does not summarize the ideas of the previous speaker.
e. When the timer goes off, discuss your feelings about the activity. What was hard? What did you like? What did you not like? Also listen to the time keeper's comments.
f. Switch roles and repeat.

Only the Best Intentions

READ THE SCRIPT

Read the play. Make notes. Then discuss the questions that follow.

The play takes place in a modern city where different family members find themselves faced with changing expectations regarding marriage and family roles. It explores the question, "What can people expect from a 21st century marriage?"

CAST

Fiona Curry: (early 40s) Gigi and Jaime's mother. She is a working mother who does her best to take care of her kids. She's especially supportive of Jaime's soccer career.

Paulo Curry: (mid 40s) Gigi and Jaime's father. He is an accountant. He is devoted to his family. He enjoys having them around and tries to make them happy.

Jaime Curry: (15) Their youngest son. He is a skilled soccer player. Ideally, Jaime wears a soccer jersey or sports clothes.

Gigi Curry-Bao: (21) Their older daughter and fiancée of Oscar Bao. She is also devoted to family and the idea of creating one.

Miranda Curry-Fields: (mid 40s) Paulo's older sister. She works for an international company, and reads a lot of articles, so she feels confident about her opinions.

Oscar Bao: (23) Gigi's fiancée. He has no family in the United States. He works in a restaurant and plays video games in his spare time. This is a habit he picked up before he met Gigi.

Mimi Curry: (early 60s) Gigi's grandmother. Paulo and Miranda's mother. She is the matriarch (center of the family).

Baba Curry: (mid 60s) Gigi's grandfather. A retired store owner and soccer fan.

Note: The family is multicultural. The Currys are immigrants to an English-speaking country. Mimi and Baba live in the home country but visit often. Oscar is also an immigrant. He originally came with his parents, but they returned. The cast can decide which countries the characters are from and change names appropriately.

OTHER ROLES

Director – Organizes the cast and facilitates table work, including script changes, helps actors with their motivations and relationships, guides the blocking.
Stage manager – Responsible for sound effects, turning off the lights between scenes, providing cues as necessary etc.
Videographer – Videos and edits a digital version of the production. The videographer might also work with others to make a documentary of the production process.

Cast and crew can also take on assignments for helping with costumes and set including finding props and changing the scenery as needed. Some participants might also like to design a poster and/or create a program with photos and short biographies of the cast members and their roles.

Scene 1: *It is a weekday morning at the Curry household. Fiona is in the kitchen/dining area of her family home. There is a table, a laptop, and maybe a coffee cup. She is pacing and talking on the phone.*

Fiona: Jaime missed the bus again.

(*Pause*)

I thought you were taking care of it.

(*Pause*)

I was, but the repair guy is coming.

(*Pause*)

For the dishwasher. I told you.

(*Pause*)

I know, but I can't leave. He'll be here any minute.

(*Pause*)

I know you can't. So . . . what do you want to do?

(*Jaime walks in. He has a phone in his hand.*)

Jaime: It's fine mom, I'll go by Uber.

Fiona: Hang on a minute. (*Turns to Jaime*) You have an Uber app? When did you get that?

Jaime: A while ago. It's fine. I got this.

Fiona: (*Into phone*) He says he'll Uber. Is that okay? (*Pause*) Okay then. (*Nods at Jaime*)

(*Jaime starts to leave.*)

Wait! Jaime, do you have your soccer shoes?

Jaime: Yes, right here. And my socks.

Fiona: Okay then. Have a good practice! (*Turns and attends to the phone*) I've got a Skype call with a client in a few minutes. I gotta go.

(*Pause*)

Okay, can we talk about it later?

(*Pause*)

And don't forget you have to pick up your parents at the airport on Friday! Yes, the meet-the-family thing for Gigi and Oscar.

(*Pause*)

At your sister's. Yes! Miranda's got it all planned. All you have to do is go to the airport and pick up your parents.

(*Pause*)

Paulo, I told you all this yesterday! Remember we talked about how nice it was for Miranda to plan this party? Oscar doesn't have any family in the U.S.! We are his family now. We need to make him feel welcome, so yes, you have to come.

(*Gigi walks in looking upset. Fiona is still on the phone. Gigi stops and looks at her mother. Fiona sees her and holds up a finger.*)

Fiona: Paulo, I gotta go, uh-huh . . . bye. (*Hangs up the phone and looks at Gigi*) Gigi?

Gigi: Mommy!

Fiona: What is it? What happened?

Gigi: I've broken up with Oscar! (*Wipes away tears*)

Fiona: But . . . you've only been engaged for 3 weeks!

Gigi: (*Sits down*) I know, but it was a huge mistake. It's over!

Fiona: Oh, Gigi. (*Looks at her watch*) Do you want to talk about it?

Gigi: Can you, Mommy?

Fiona: You're my daughter. Of course I can. . . . For 15 minutes?

Gigi: I don't know what to do! We had so many plans.

Fiona: Tell me. What has my future son-in-law done?

Gigi: He's a computer addict. That's what he's done. He only cares about his stupid game.

Fiona: Oh, honey, I'm so sorry.

Gigi: Do you know he gets up at five o'clock in the morning to play with people in Korea?

Fiona: Korea? How do you know?

Gigi: Jaime told me.

(*Fiona frowns*)

Yeah! It makes me so mad! So that means he's too tired to go running. We were supposed to run six miles last Saturday, and Oscar didn't show up.

Fiona: Oh, Gigi.

Gigi: Yeah, and then we were supposed to meet to talk about the wedding, and I'm at the coffee shop, and again he's not there. I text him. No response. Then finally I get a text. He says he'll be there in a minute. He just has to finish his game. I was so mad I left without telling him.

Fiona: Oh dear. (*Gently*) And you didn't know this before you got engaged?

Gigi: I mean I knew he played computer games, but we talked about it. I thought he was going to change!

Fiona: And he didn't?

Gigi: Noooo.

Scene 2: *No set. Miranda and Fiona are on opposite sides of the stage talking on the phone.*

Miranda: Fiona! You aren't driving, are you?

Fiona: No, just working. But I'm glad you called. I was just about to call you.

Miranda: Good. I want to talk to you about Saturday.

Fiona: Me too!

Miranda: I can't do it.

Fiona: What do you mean? Everyone's supposed to meet Oscar. Your parents are coming tomorrow.

Miranda: I have a work thing . . . in Singapore.

Fiona: Singapore?

Miranda: Yeah, my boss is sending me to Singapore. But don't worry, I've made it very easy for you. All you need to do is pick up the food and take it to your house. I'll be back Sunday, so I can help with everything. I promise!

Fiona: I can't do it at my house. The repairs aren't finished.

Miranda: Okay, my house then. How about Paulo. Can he bring the stuff?

Fiona: He's picking up your parents at the airport. Anyway, don't worry about it. I think you can call off the party. Gigi's fighting with Oscar! She showed up at the house this morning, says she's breaking off the engagement.

Miranda: What? I mean I saw this coming. But I didn't think it would happen so soon!

Fiona: Gigi says he plays computer games too much.

Miranda: (*Smugly*) Well I'm not surprised. He's highly ranked, right?

Fiona: What's that? Highly ranked? I don't even know what that means.

Miranda: It means he's really good. He's played a lot of games and leveled up. And that means he's been spending a lot of time practicing.

Fiona: Really? I wasn't really paying attention.

Miranda: So I read an article about this on the plane the other day. You know that once someone is addicted to computer games, it's like a drug? People die in front of computers. They don't eat. They don't sleep. They just die.

Fiona: Oh, it can't be that bad! He's still working at the restaurant. They've got plans to open their own place.

Miranda: I'm just sayin' . . . He's been on his own for a long time, and you, yourself, said Gigi is upset.

Fiona: Yeah, she is. But I figure they'll talk and work it out. And if that fails, I'm calling in your mother. If she can't fix it, I don't know who can.

Miranda: Oh yeah, Mimi's good at family stuff.

Fiona: Oh yeah. Poor Oscar. You know he doesn't have any family. He'll be lost without Gigi.

Miranda: I know. But Gigi's got to take care of herself. This computer game thing could be worse than you think!

Fiona: I don't know.

Miranda: Maybe it's for the best. She quit college when she got engaged, didn't she? Maybe she can go back.

Scene 3: *Late afternoon. Jaime is lying on the floor doing homework with ear buds. He picks up his phone, squints, takes a photo, and posts it on Snapchat. His father Paulo walks in.*

Paulo: That you, Jaime?

Jaime: Yeah.

Paulo: (*Sits*) So, how was school?

Jaime: Fine.

Paulo: Did you Uber?

Jaime: (*Takes out one earbud*) Yep.

Paulo: Good. Did you get to practice on time?

Jaime: Uh-huh.

Paulo: Where's your mother?

Jaime: She was here.

Paulo: She left?

Jaime: I don't know.

Paulo: I need to talk to her. Do you know where she went?

Jaime: She didn't say.

Paulo: Miranda called me.

Jaime: Aunt Miranda? (*Sighs and sits up. He takes out the other earbud.*)

Paulo: Yeah, she wants to have the meet-the-family thing here.

Jaime: I thought it was going to be at her house. She has the pool and everything.

Paulo: Apparently, she has to go to Malaysia or some place, like, for work.

Jaime: Not Malaysia, Singapore.

Paulo: Singapore?

Jaime: Yeah, a sales meeting.

Paulo: Anyway, she wants me to talk to your mom about it.

Jaime: Mom's said no. It has to be at her house. Oh, and Gigi's here.

Paulo: Gigi? What's she doing here?

(*Gigi enters. She is still hurt and angry with Oscar.*)

Gigi: Hi, Dad! (*Looks at her phone*)

Paulo: Hi, Gigi. What's up?

Jaime: Gigi left Oscar.

Paulo: (*Shocked*) Wait, wait, wait a sec. What? What?

Jaime: She's not going to marry Oscar. She changed her mind.

Paulo: You can't do this, Gigi. What will people think? Your grandparents are flying halfway across the world to meet him!

(*Gigi shrugs*)

Paulo: You just need to talk to Oscar. I'm sure you can work it out.

Gigi: You don't understand, Dad. He doesn't love me. He only loves Epic Storm.

Paulo: What's Epic Storm.

Jaime: It's a computer game. Oscar's got a super-high ranking.

Paulo: A computer game? You're leaving him because of a computer game?

Gigi: It's more like *he's* leaving *me* for a computer game. I mean, that's what's happening basically. It's the only thing he cares about.

Paulo: He's leaving you, for a computer game? I don't get it.

Gigi: I have been a complete idiot!

Paulo: What did he do?

Gigi: He didn't *do* anything. That's the problem. He just has other priorities. He would rather play Epic Storm than live in the real world with me.

Jaime: (*Trying to be helpful*) Well I kind of understand. Epic Storm *is* kind of addictive! Not trying to take his side or anything, but it's a really fun game.

Gigi: You are taking his side!

Jaime: No, I'm just saying giving up Epic Storm would be a huge sacrifice. Like I said, he's highly ranked.

Gigi: So he can be married to Epic Storm! I'm not going to compete with a computer game!

Paulo: Let me talk to him. I can fix this.

Gigi: No, Dad.

Paulo: (*Takes out his phone*) I'm going to call him. We'll get him to come over. We'll sit down and we'll sort this all out.

Gigi: No, Daddy! I know you mean well, but it's not going to work.

Paulo: You don't mean that.

Gigi: (*Getting more agitated*) I do mean that! Nobody believes me, but I'm done with that man.

Jaime: (*Looks at his phone*) Oscar just texted me. He wants you to call him, Gigi.

Gigi: Tell him I'm not available.

(*Jaime texts. Paulo's phone rings. He answers it*)

Paulo: Hi Oscar. Yes, she's here. Just a sec. (*Turns to Gigi and holds out the phone*) It's Oscar. He wants to talk to you.

(*Gigi leaves the room*)

Paulo: Um, I thought she was here. (*Looks at Jaime and gestures as if he doesn't know what to say*) Jaime, didn't you say she was here? (*Turns back to phone*) She was here a second ago.

(*Pause*)

Yes, I'll tell her to call you. (*Hangs up. Then he calls to Gigi who is offstage.*) Gigi? Oscar's sorry. He loves you **Gigi** (*from offstage*) I'm not speaking to him!

Scene 4: *The next day. Oscar's apartment. Oscar is lower stage right. He has a headset on and he's playing on a keyboard while looking at a monitor. There is an open chip bag and a soda can next to him and a plastic or paper bag in the corner. Jaime walks stage left and knocks on an imaginary door (He can tap the ground with his shoe, or the stage manager can provide the audio). Oscar ignores the knock. Jaime knocks again, and Oscar lifts his headphone off one ear and goes back to the game. Jaime takes out his phone and calls. Oscar sees his phone light up and swipes it with his finger.*

Oscar: (*To phone*) Hey, can you wait just a second? I'm almost done.

Jaime: (*Speaking into his phone*) Yeah, sure. (*Begins to scroll on his phone*)

Oscar: (*Continuing his game*) Okay. (*Leans forward and punches some keys in the final moments. Then he gets agitated and talks to his screen.*) Monkey, monkey, monkey, look out! Whoa, what a move (*Exhales in relief and exhilaration*) Whooff! (*Moves the mouse and hits keys. He is excited. Then he raises his hands in victory and leans back in his chair*) That was awesome, Reg! Okay, I gotta go. Someone is at the door. (*Gets up and opens the door. Jaime is still looking at his phone, finishing a thread.*)

Oscar: Hey there.

Jaime: Hi, Oscar.

Oscar: Come in.

Jaime: (*Finishing his text*) Thanks.

Oscar: The drone is over there.

Jaime: Great! (*Comes in and picks up the bag. He stands there awkwardly for a minute.*) Thanks for letting us borrow it. My dad can't come to the game, so he's really happy we can make a video.

Oscar: No worries. I haven't used it in a while. You might need to charge it.

Jaime: Okay. Everything's here, right?

Oscar: Yeah... So, uh, how's it going? (Oscar *does some wrist stretches. He holds his arm straight out and then uses the other hand to pull his fingers back to stretch the wrist muscles, once up, once down. This is something he has to do to stay in shape for gaming.*)

Jaime: You mean how's it going with me? Or how's it going with Gigi?

Oscar: Gigi. Does everyone at your house hate me? (*Switches to stretch the other wrist*)

Jaime: Not everybody.

Oscar: What did Gigi say?

Jaime: She thinks you're addicted to Epic Storm. She's pretty angry.

Oscar: I tried to call her. She won't answer.

Jaime: Yeah, I know.

Oscar: She'll come back.

Jaime: You think?

Oscar: (*Begins to pace*) I don't know. The problem is Gigi doesn't understand that I'm in the middle of a tournament. I can't just quit!

Jaime: I know. I watched your game last night on Twitch. You were awesome. Congrats!

Oscar: Thanks! Did you say anything to Gigi about it?

Jaime: No, why? Should I have?

Oscar: (*Disappointed*) I guess not. She wouldn't have cared.

Jaime: Maybe not.

Oscar: She'd just say it's stupid.

Jaime: Uh-huh. (*Pause*) Well, I better go. (*Walks toward the door and begins to open it. He is interrupted by Oscar who wants to talk.*)

Oscar: I would walk through fire for your sister! But I don't think *she* cares about *me*! All she does is hate on my gaming.

Jaime: Well, she loves you.

Oscar: Well, what do I do now?

Jaime: I wouldn't know. I'm only 15. To me, you have a great life on your own! Gaming as much as you want, eating chips for dinner . . .

Oscar: It's not all great!

Jaime: Well, you might not be able to have it both ways. Maybe it's best to get away now. (*Starts to leave again*) Make a clean break from the crazy Currys while you can.

Oscar: But . . . wait. What if I don't want a clean break?

Jaime: You really want to know?

Oscar: Yeah, I do.

Jaime: (*Turns and speaks hesitantly*) Well . . . Here's the thing. Don't take this wrong way, but I've been thinking about it. Maybe you guys aren't playing by the same rules.

Oscar: What do you mean? Here, don't go. Sit down!

Jaime: (*Still standing*) It's kind of like you've broken the rules.

Oscar: (*Frustrated*) What rules?

Jaime: Well, let's say your relationship is like a soccer game. You've got to follow the rules, right? You can't go offside. You can't hurt people. If you hurt someone, you get a yellow card. Maybe Gigi has just handed you a yellow card.

Oscar: Red card, more like . . .

Jaime: Well, red card then. You ignored her and hurt her feelings, so you're out of the game. You've broken the rules.

Oscar: Well what about my rules? How come she's not following my rules.

Jaime: Well, it seems like she hasn't broken *your* rules. *You've* broken *her* rules, though.

Oscar: Yeahhhh.

Jaime: So you didn't give her a red card. She gave you one. You can't control that.

Oscar: I hate to say it, but I think you're right.

Jaime: It's just a thought. But I really gotta go. If I don't keep my grades up, I'm off the team.

Oscar: Okay. I understand.

Jaime: Thanks, see ya.

Oscar: Bye.

(*Jaime leaves. Oscar turns and looks at his empty room. He pauses. Then he goes to the computer, sits. Another pause. Then he puts on the headset.*)

Scene 5: *A few days later. Miranda's house, the living room. The stage is empty.*

Paulo: (*Offstage*) Here we are, Mimi! Let me find the key. Here it is. We'll be inside in just a second. Watch your step.

(*The grandparents, Baba and Mimi, enter followed by Paulo, who is carrying the suitcase.*)

Mimi: I don't understand why we are here. Why don't you just put us in a motel. We'll be fine.

Paulo: Miranda and I wouldn't think of it. Miranda's flight gets here in a couple of hours, and she wants to see you.

(*Baba looks around the kitchen.*)

Mimi: Oh, for heaven's sake! Paulo, your father needs a chair.

Paulo: (*Pulls out a chair*) Baba, sit down. What can I get you? Tea? Water?

Mimi: A cup of tea would be perfect. I tell you! That airplane was crowded. Baba couldn't get out of his seat. I felt like a piece of cheese in a sandwich.

Baba: That's right. Like a piece of cheese in a sandwich! A grilled cheese sandwich! It was hot too.

Mimi: It was awful. Now, where's my Gigi?

(*Gigi enters*)

Gigi: Mimi! (*Runs to her and gives her a hug*)

Mimi: My baby girl! Look at you! Pretty as ever!

Gigi: No, I'm not. I'm a mess.

Baba: Your father told us you are having a few problems with your fiancée.

Gigi: You could say that. I thought I was getting a husband, but it looks like I'm marrying a computer with a human attached to it.

Mimi: Tsk-tsk. Yes, leave him. You don't need that.

Gigi: (*Surprised*) You agree with me?

Mimi: Of course I do! You're too good for him. Go back to college!

Gigi: That's what Aunt Miranda says. Has she been talking to you? (*Suspiciously*) Did she say something bad about Oscar? She never liked him.

Mimi: (*Ignoring the question*) Gigi. Come on. Let's make a cup of tea and you can tell me all about it.

(*Gigi and Mimi go off stage.*)

Paulo: What is Mimi doing?

Baba: You know your mother. She has a goal.

Paulo: Yes, I do. That's why I'm asking. Is she up to something?

Baba: She's always up to something.

(*Fiona enters*)

Ah, here's Fiona. Hi Fiona.

Fiona: (*In a rush*) Hi Baba. It's so good to see you! How was your flight? Do you want to rest? I'm sorry we don't have any food. Miranda's been out of town, and I've been . . . Well, it doesn't matter. We can order out. Paulo, call for a pizza or something.

Paulo: I hate pizza.

Baba: I'm fine. Just being with my family is enough.

Fiona: Jaime will be here in a minute. (*Proudly*) He has some news.

Paulo: Did he win?

Fiona: I don't know. You'll have to ask him.

(*Jaime enters*)

Jaime: Hey Baba! Good to see you! (*Shakes hands with Baba*)

Baba: My gosh, boy. You are so big and strong. I can't believe it.

Jaime: You just saw me six months ago.

Baba: And you were a tiny, skinny thing.

Fiona: And now he's a big, tall, skinny thing. He doesn't eat!

(*Mimi and Gigi enter with a tray of tea—this can be imaginary*)

Mimi: I'll say. Jaime, what did they do to you? Put you in a stretching machine?

Jaime: (*Smiles*) Yes, Mimi. They put me in a stretching machine.

Paulo: So, the game, the game. What happened?

Jamie: We won!

Fiona: But there's more. Tell them, Jaime.

Jamie: I scored.

Fiona: Twice! We won 3 to 2. Jamie got a pass and made the winning shot. It was so exciting! I thought I was going to die!

Baba: Unbelievable! I am so sorry we missed it.

Paulo: Well we can watch it later! Did you get the video?

Fiona: Yes. Yes, It's right here on my flash drive.

(*Everyone crowds around Jaime talking at once, saying things like, "That's great", "Congratulations!", "Good job", etc. Suddenly Oscar enters with two food bags or boxes. Baba sees him first and steps back. The others notice, and they all turn around. There is silence as Oscar stands there with food looking at Gigi. Gigi takes a step back and folds her arms. There is a pause.*)

Fiona: Oscar!

Scene 6: *Miranda's house, an hour later. Gigi is sitting alone on a stool or step, facing the audience. Oscar comes to the doorway wiping his hands as if he's been washing up.*

Oscar: Everyone's eaten. Aren't you hungry?

Gigi: (*Still upset*) No thanks.

Oscar: Gigi, can we talk?

Gigi: But . . . don't you have a game or a tournament or something?

Oscar: No, no.

(*Gigi shrugs. Oscar sits next to her. Both are turned toward the audience but do not make eye contact with the audience.*)

Gigi: Mimi says I should go back to college.

Oscar: That's a good idea.

Gigi: You think so?

Oscar: Sure. I think it's a great idea. You're the smartest person I've ever met!

Gigi: Really?

Oscar: I want you to be happy, Gigi. It's just complicated.

Gigi: Are you sure. Because it's not that complicated to me. I thought we had a plan. We were going to work hard, save money, and open Oscar and Gigi's Cafe.

Oscar: We can, but it's just, maybe, not a good time right now. I have this tournament.

Gigi: The tournament. There is always a tournament, Oscar, isn't there.

Oscar: Gigi, it was not my intention for any of this to happen. I was just playing for fun, you know? And then Reg asked me to fill in for a guy, and one thing led to another, and I couldn't let the team down. I didn't think we'd make it this far.

Gigi: It's just a game. What is so important about a game?

Oscar: Actually, I need to tell you something, Gigi. It's not just a game. I am starting to realize that it's more than that. I can't help it.

Gigi: Seriously? Do you think you are addicted?

Oscar: It's not that. It's not like I have to do it. I want to spend time with you. It just feels like I have this ability to be really good, like I want to see how far I can go.

Gigi: In Epic Storm?

Oscar: Yes. You know how everyone is so proud of Jaime. He's great at soccer, and he deserves it. But how Jaime feels about soccer, I feel about gaming. Only everyone hates me for it.

Gigi: Okay, but soccer is a sport.

Oscar: So is Epic Storm. It's an esport.

Gigi: I'm sorry, Oscar. Really?

Oscar: I'm going to L.A., Gigi.

Gigi: What?

Oscar: Yes, for the finals. We won the last round, and for the finals we get to play in an auditorium. The company is paying for everything. There will be commentators, sponsors, everything. It's actually kind of a big deal!

Gigi: Wow! That's big. You didn't tell me.

Oscar: You wouldn't talk to me.

Gigi: You're serious?

Oscar: Yes, I just found out.

Gigi: But you're a cook. A really good cook! Are you giving all that up?

Oscar: I'm an okay cook, maybe a good cook. But what if it turns out I'm a *great* gamer?

Gigi: What do you mean?

Oscar: What if I could win a lot of money? It could lead to a career.

Gigi: Really? So now you want to be a professional gamer?

Oscar: Well, there's a chance. And I want to take it.

Gigi: Oscar, you should. It's your dream. (*Gets up and looks directly at Oscar*) But it's not mine. (*She leaves. Oscar watches her go. Then he takes out his phone.*)

Scene 7: *The airport a few days later. Miranda, Paulo, Jaime, Gigi, Baba, and Mimi walk on stage with rolling suitcases and boarding passes. They are one big, united family.*

Baba: (*Urgently*) Where are the B gates?

Mimi: Over there, dear. We have to go through the security check, first.

Paulo: We have to say goodbye here, Baba.

Baba: Do you think we have to take off our shoes? I don't want to take off my shoes. I think there's a hole in my sock.

Mimi: I thought I threw those socks away!

Baba: Well, they were my last clean socks. I could wear dirty socks or socks with a hole. What was I supposed to do?

Miranda: It'll be fine, Baba. No one will be looking at your socks.

Mimi: (*Turns to Jaime*) We'll be back in a few months. Maybe this time we can see you play, Jaime.

Jaime: (*Nods*) Okay. I'll try not to get injured.

Fiona: And he'll keep his grades up, right Jaime?

Baba: Let's go Mimi. I don't want to miss the plane.

Mimi: (*Turns to Gigi*) You okay Gigi?

Miranda: Gigi's fine! She's going to put all this behind her, aren't you, honey.

Gigi: I don't know. (*Pause*) Mimi, I see you and Baba, and you seem so . . . so comfortable. I want that. I want that big crazy happy family thing. I just thought Oscar wanted it too.

Mimi: Oh, it wasn't always like this. I used to get so angry with your grandfather! I broke up with him four times before we got married!

Baba: No, you didn't!

Mimi: Yes, I did. You just don't remember. It was the only way to get you to listen!

Baba: Four times?

Mimi: Yes!

Gigi: You did that? Is that normal?

Mimi: Sure. (*Looks at Baba*) But I always took him back. (*Winks*) It works every time. It'll work for you too. You'll see. Oscar will quit his game.

Baba: (*Looks at his watch*) Mimi, we've gotta go!

Mimi: Don't look so sad, Gigi. It's going to be okay.

(*Gigi waves goodbye. Oscar walks on stage behind her, also holding a boarding pass. Gigi turns and sees him. The rest see the couple and move off stage.*)

Gigi: You?

Oscar: I got here a little early. I hoped I might see you.

Gigi: Oh . . . On your way to L.A. then?

Oscar: Yep. They're picking me up at the airport, limo, and everything.

Gigi: Wow.

Oscar: Can I call you when I get there?

Gigi: Sure, yeah, or text, you know, just so I know you're safe.

Oscar: I'm a little nervous. It would be nice to hear your voice.

Gigi: Really?

Oscar: Yes, really.

Gigi: (*Not angry anymore*) Okay, I'd like that. (*Pause*) Also, Oscar, I've been thinking. Maybe it's a mistake to plan out our lives right now.

Oscar: (*Thinks she's breaking up*) Yeah. I get it. I've been expecting too much.

Gigi: Well, yeah.

Oscar: Sooo (*Turns and reluctantly starts to walk away.*)

Gigi: Mimi thinks if I push you away, you'll do anything to get me back.

Oscar: (*Turns back, hopeful*) But I will! I *will* do anything. I can give up gaming.

Gigi: Oh, like that's going to happen. (*She gestures toward Oscar and his bag.*) Look at you. You're on your way to L.A.!

Oscar: Well I can't give it up at this moment, but . . .

Gigi: (*Interrupts*) Oscar, we can't keep doing this.

Oscar: (*Resigned*) Yeah, you're right.

Gigi: But maybe we can find a different way.

Oscar: I'm confused. Are you saying maybe we *can* get married? Or we *can't*? Or, what *are* you saying?

Gigi: I don't know. I thought you wanted to open a restaurant together, but you don't.

Oscar: Well, it was an idea. . . . something to talk about.

Gigi: Yeah, fun to talk about, but maybe not commit to. Oscar, I've realized something. I'm still young. I'm only 20. I don't even know what I want.

Oscar: Wow! That's a relief. I was just doing the restaurant plan because I thought you wanted to.

Gigi: And I was doing it because I thought you wanted to. I thought it was something we could do together.

Oscar: Honestly, I am actually not that into being a chef, and I have no problem with you going back to college. You're so smart, Gigi. You should.

Gigi: Thanks, Oscar. That means a lot to me.

(*Oscar nods then looks up startled as Paulo, Miranda, Jaime, and Fiona appear and stand behind Gigi.*)

Gigi: I'm willing to try something, too. Can you tell me how to get online to see your game?

Oscar: Yeah, I guess so. Why?

Gigi: I want to watch your Epic Storm tournament.

Oscar: You really want to? (*Hopeful*) You might like it. There's a whole story with heroes and magic. (*Turns to Jaime*) Jaime, can you show her?

Jaime: Sure. We can watch it together.

Gigi: I can't promise I'll like it. But if it's important to you maybe I can learn about it. . . . Just a little bit.

Oscar: Then there's hope?

Gigi: Yes, I was really hurt when you got into that tournament thing. I felt like it was more important to you than me. But what can I do? I care about you, and you love this, so I have to accept it. Maybe if I understand it, then . . .

Oscar: Then what?

Gigi: Then I can be happy for you. And I want to be happy for you. I don't know what that means for the future, but I'm willing to try.

Fiona: We all want the best for you, Oscar!

Gigi: Thanks, Mom!

Paulo: She's right. We'll all watch your game. That's what we Currys do! We stick together.

Oscar: (*Smiles*) Wow, I am so relieved! I didn't want to lose you! (*Looks at Gigi, then the rest of the family.*) Any of you!

Jaime: This is going to be so funny! You guys don't know the first thing about Epic Storm.

Miranda: Does it matter?

Jaime: I guess not.

Paulo: We'll figure it out. Now come on, Baba and Mimi have a plane to catch! Oscar, do you have time to walk over with us?

Oscar: Absolutely!

(*The family all walk off stage united.*)

[Curtain]

DISCUSSION

Talk about the play in groups. Share your analysis with the class.

1. What is the problem with Oscar and Gigi's relationship at the beginning of the play?
2. How are the family's feelings about Jaime's soccer different from their feelings about Oscar's sport?
3. How does the story reflect the background readings about families and screens?
4. Who changes during the play? How do they change?
5. What ideas do you think the audience should take away from this play?

Production

Perform your play for your class or another class. You may also choose to video your play. Here are some suggestions for rehearsing and performing.

- **Rehearsed reading:** Actors work with a director and the script. They sit or stand in one place. Then they read the parts with a focus on emotion, stress, and intonation.
- **Staged reading (also called Reader's Theater):** Actors work with a director and the script. They also block the play. They perform just like in a real theatre. However, in the performance, they carry and read from a script.
- **Full performance:** Actors prepare their roles, memorize their lines, and block the play. They perform for an audience just like in a real theatre. There can be an intermission in which audience members can reflect or ask questions, or the play can continue to the end.
- **Video:** Work with a videographer to record the performance and then edit the video. Watch it later with your teacher, your group, or the whole class.

For resources on ways to perform the play, go to http://www.alphabetpublishingbooks.com/integrated-skills-through-drama.

ANALYZE THE PLAY

Re-read the play silently. Answer the questions by taking a few notes on your own. Then discuss your answers in a group.

The Story	Notes
The main characters of a story always have a conflict. Who are the main characters in this story, and what is their conflict?	
A play often deals with a serious social issue. What is the social issue in this play? What groups in society are affected by it?	

Even a serious play can have comic moments. Comedy often appears in family drama because audience members recognize their own experiences in the characters. For example, a family cannot see a truth that is obvious to others. In what way is this play funny?	
A play should be believable. The audience should empathize with one or more characters. Do you feel similar to any of the people in the play? Explain.	

ASSIGN ROLES

Decide who will play which character. There are two ways to do this.

- Give the director/teacher the names of two or three characters you are willing to play. Then that person will assign you a role.
- Audition for a part. Audition for a part. Read one scene with another student as one or more characters. The director/teacher assigns roles to people who are the best fit.

LEARN YOUR PART

Read the play again and highlight your lines in yellow. Then make decisions about your character's personality and emotions. Write notes next to your lines.

a. Read the vocabulary describing emotional states and the first example. Write a second example from your own experience or research.

	Example one	*Example two*
defensive	Lee says I'm a bad roommate when I tell him he is addicted to computer games.	
distracted	Hector is talking on the phone and typing while Esme is trying to ask him a question.	

	Example one	*Example two*
distressed	Amelia's car is gone. She doesn't know if the police took it or someone stole it.	
dramatic	Ivan announces his love for Natasha in front of many people.	
gentle	Lily tells Ben it is not his fault when she gives him the bad news about his pet.	
humble	Jan says, "I was not that great. It was my teammates who made this win possible."	
hurt	Tai's friend did not recommend him for a spot on the team.	
proud	Kemo is very happy about his son's academic achievements.	
in denial	My grandfather cannot hear me, but he refuses to get a hearing aid.	
indignant	Cami is 8 years old, and she gets upset when people think she is only 6.	
resigned	Tran stops trying to get his brother to help with the housework.	
smug	Reza says, "I told you so! I knew that would happen! But no one believed me."	
tentative	Peng cannot guess Linh's feelings, so he is very careful when he talks to her.	

PLAY ON EMOTIONS

Develop your acting (and communication) skills through this simple game.

Prepare: Get in groups of four or five and review the emotional states vocabulary above. Practice saying sentences in the manner of a specific emotion from the list. For example, say, "He's not coming. He's playing a computer game," in a resigned way, or, "Gigi called off the wedding" in a way that shows you are happy.

Play

1. Get in groups of 3 or 4. Take turns. Speaker A chooses an emotion word from the list but does not reveal the word to the other players.
2. A timekeeper set a clock for two minutes.
3. Speaker A reads one of the sentences below. He or she uses body language gesture and voice to communicate the emotion. The speaker may read the sentence more than once within the two minutes.
4. Other members of the group try to guess the emotion. The person who guesses the emotion gets a point.
5. Speaker B takes a turn. The game continues until all people in the group have been speaker or the time for the game is up.

Sentences

Note that these sentences can communicate a variety of emotions. It's your voice and gesture that will show how you feel when you say them.

1. He's not coming. He's playing a computer game.
2. They're leaving for Los Angeles in the morning.
3. Gigi called off the wedding.
4. I can't help it. I didn't ask to be in the tournament.
5. I told you about Jamie's game. You just don't remember.
6. All the relatives are coming.
7. I knew that would happen.
8. Oscar is on the phone.
9. You always say that!

b. Decide how your character feels in your scenes and use the vocabulary from the chart above or your own ideas to make notes on your script.

c. Memorize your lines. Choose from the following strategies. It will take several rehearsals to remember everything. Overlearn your part so you do not forget later.

- Read your part out loud two or three times a day.
- Record yourself saying the lines. Listen to the recording and try to improve your pronunciation, speed, and volume. You'll need to speak loudly and clearly in performance.
- Read while standing. Think about your movements and your tone of voice.
- Read with a friend who can say the other characters' lines.

REHEARSE

Read the play with other actors, and talk about your characters' relationships.

a. Use the sentence stems below or your own ideas to discuss your motivations.

In this scene,

I want to hide my true feelings.	I need some attention.
You are expecting too much, and I feel upset.	I want to explain my point of view, but I am afraid of the reaction.
I would like you to stay and talk to me.	I kind of like arguing about this.
I am enjoying this drama! It makes me feel alive.	I'm telling you a secret.
I mean the opposite of what I say.	I'm accepting something I did not want to believe.
I want you to feel guilty.	I'm sharing something very important to me.

b. Review pragmatics After your rehearsal, answer the questions below. Then discuss your notes with the group.

1. How do other characters respond to you? Does it feel natural?

2. How do your pragmatics choices make the play funny or serious? Try saying something with a different emotion. Use different stress patterns, gesture, and voice until you feel comfortable with your message.

3. What phrases or expressions do characters use to signal their feelings? For example, *I saw this coming* is an expression people use when they have warned others but no one listened.

4. Would you make the same language choices if you were in this situation in your life?

> ### *Improv*
>
> *Improv* is short for improvisation or the art of making something up on the spot, without planning. In theatre, improv is about finding humor or meaning in a roleplay. Improv activities help actors discover their characters by acting out scenes without a script. The actors pretend to be their characters and they make up the conversations.
>
> Through improv they can:
>
> - get to know their character's personality better
> - understand their character's relationships with other characters
> - be *in the moment* so the scene feels like real people talking to each other
> - discover the physical mannerisms of their character (For example, an important woman might flick her eyes at someone's feet before looking at their eyes as a way to show power)
> - overcome stage fright and get comfortable in front of an audience

c. **Improvise a scene** Choose a situation for your improv from the list below or make up your own idea. Set a timer for 2 minutes and perform your improv for another group or the class.

- Gigi and Jaime have a conversation about gaming. Jaime tries to explain why it's fun, and Gigi moves from hating it to understanding it.
- Miranda talks to Fiona about computer game addiction. She thinks Oscar can't change, but Fiona thinks he can.
- Mimi and Gigi have a conversation about marriage. Mimi believes Gigi should make Oscar choose between Epic Storm and marriage. Gigi is not so sure. She might even want to defend Oscar.
- Oscar, Baba, and Paulo talk about sports. Oscar tries to explain how esports are like traditional sports. Baba disagrees, but Paulo is interested.

PRACTICE PRONUNCIATION

Work on finding the right stress and intonation. Also identify and practice any specific sounds that you have trouble with.

Sentence Stress to Clarify and Show Contrast

In English, people say content words such as nouns, verbs, and adjectives, and some adverbs louder and longer than function words like prepositions and articles. When correcting a person's misunderstanding or expressing strong emotions, they may give extra emphasis.

Here are some examples from the play. The **bold** type indicates words that are stressed.

*That's what he's **done**. He only cares about his **stupid** game.*

*People **die** in front of computers. They don't **eat**. They don't **sleep**. They just **die**.*

*You're leaving him because of a **computer** game?*

*It's more like **he's** leaving **me**.*

*. . . it seems like **she** hasn't broken **your** rules. **You've** broken **her** rules, though.*

*Are you saying maybe we **can** get married? Or we **can't**? Or, what **are** you saying?*

Go over your lines and mark nouns, verbs, adjectives, and adverbs that you want to stress. Pay careful attention to places where you contrast information or correct a misunderstanding.

Pronunciation and linking

In the stress and intonation patterns of English, people often link words, particularly words that are not stressed. Sometimes two or three words can sound like only one word. Practicing linking will help you sound more like a native speaker and also keep the emphasis on the important words in a sentence. In the examples below the undertie (‿) show where people link words. Here are two common ways that linking occurs.

- when a vowel sound at the beginning of a word attaches to a consonant sound at the end of the previous word.

    I like‿it. Something to talk‿about I have‿an‿idea

- when the sound at the end of a word is the same as the sound at the beginning of the next word.

    I want‿that. Have a good‿day. . . . get‿to practice on time?

Read the examples from the play. Notice that linking can make it difficult for people to understand individual words, so the goal is not to *try* to link but to keep the emphasis on the stressed content word.

Have‿a **good practice**!
and I'm‿at‿the **coffee shop**, and‿**again** he's not‿there
Hey, can‿you **wait** just‿a **second**?
I'm‿in the **middle**‿of‿a **tournament**.
He **wants**‿you to **call**‿him

It's not‿that. It's not like‿I **have** to do it. I **want**‿to **spend time** with‿you.
I'll **try** not‿to get‿**injured.**

    d. Go over your lines and mark nouns, verbs, adjectives, and adverbs that you want to stress. Also use a dictionary to check the syllable stress on longer words. Use linking to keep the stress pattern.

    e. Use a recording device such as your phone to record yourself saying the lines out loud. Listen and make adjustments to stress and linking.

    f. Practice saying your lines with the other actors in the play. Help each other with intonation, pronunciation, and stress. Speak loudly and clearly.

STAGE YOUR PLAY

Decide on how you will move during the play, where you move, and when. Also think about how your character might show feelings through gesture and posture.

Blocking a play

When a director and actors prepare for a performance, they plan where the cast will stand, sit, and move. Here are some basic guidelines that can help you create a successful performance.

- All actors should avoid speaking with their backs to the audience.
- Actors should not make eye contact with the audience.
- All actors should speak loudly and clearly, not rush through lines.
- When one actor is speaking, all other actors should look at the speaker. They should not move or attract attention in any way.
- A seated actor looking up is less powerful than a standing actor looking down.
- Actors should behave as if the story is happening to them for the first time and they are in a real conversation. Good acting is not reciting memorized lines. It is about listening and reacting to other actors with interest and emotion.

Notes on stage directions:

- Stage right means the right side of an actor who is looking at the audience. Stage left means the left side of the actor who is looking at the audience. Front and back also describe directions from the actor's position.
- To show a scene change, it is helpful to have someone turn off the lights for a few seconds.

a. Block the play with your director. Here are some ways actors communicate emotions. Try acting them out. What emotion does each of the following gestures communicate?

1. Fold your arms across your chest
2. Put your hands on their hips
3. Hold up your hands, palms outward
4. Sit and look up at a speaker/ Stand and look down at a speaker
5. Play with a phone or look away
6. Stand with a straight back
7. Stand with a bent back
8. Walk up and down the stage
9. Put your hands over your eyes or in your hair
10. Cover your mouth
11. Put your hand over your heart
12. Bow your head
13. Tilt your head to the side
14. Shake your head
15. Roll your eyes
16. Sigh loudly
17. Bite your lip
18. Make your hands into claws
19. Look at someone's feet then their face

b. Decide where you will stand and how you will move during the play. Practice several times. When you practice a lot, you will make fewer mistakes, and you will be less likely to laugh during your performance.

Note: When you are rehearsing or performing, a stage manager can sit next to the stage and read the

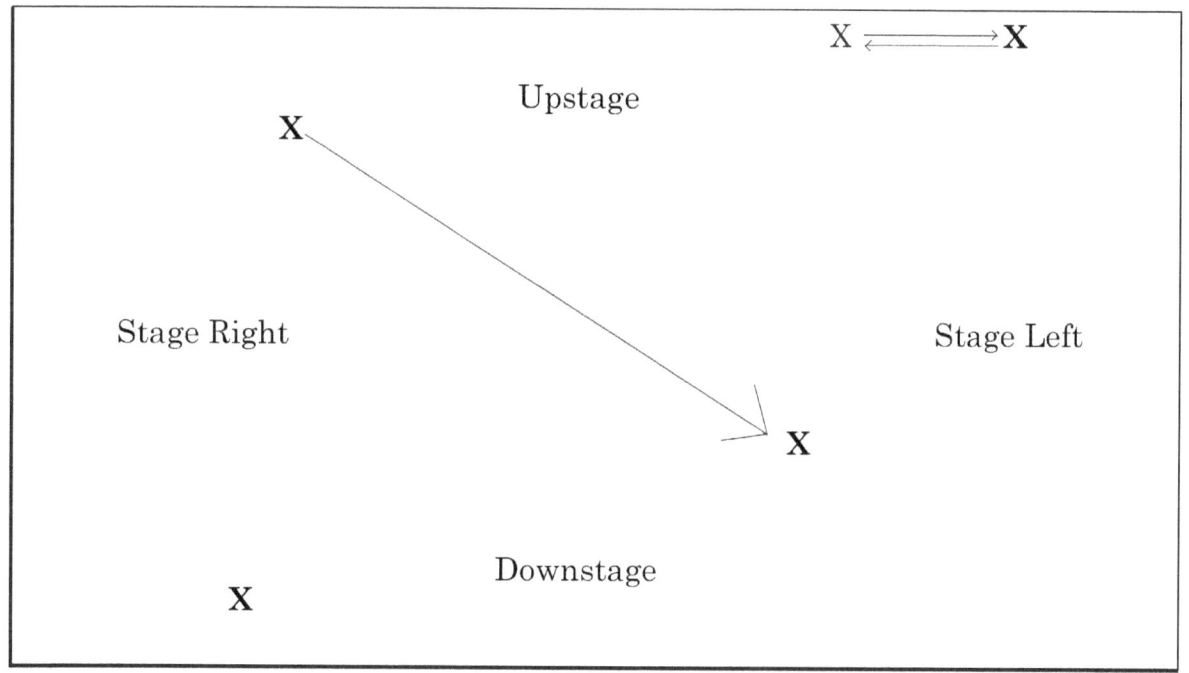

Post-Performance

 The following activities can be used to explore themes and language after a production.

LEAD A TALKBACK

The director/teacher leads the class in a conversation about the play between the actors and the audience. There are many ways to do this but the following process can help you insure a productive discussion.

    a. There is a five-minute break after the play ends while audience members take a few minutes to write some questions. Here are some examples:

- How did you prepare for your role?
- What was your character's attitude toward computer games?
- How is your own attitude toward computer games similar to or different from your character's?
- Why does Gigi change?
- How is Oscar caught between two worlds?
- What kind of message does the play communicate about gamers and esports?
- What do you think will happen between Oscar and Gigi in the future?

    b. The director and actors come out on stage and face the audience. The director invites questions and comments. The audience asks about the play or the characters. People can direct their questions to individual actors. They can also tell how the play made them feel or what it made them think about.

WRITE AN ALTERNATIVE ENDING

Break up into groups and discuss other possible endings. Answer the questions. Then write your own scene(s).

1. What happens in the new ending?
2. Why does it happen?

3. How will it affect the lives of the different people involved?
4. Which is a better ending for the characters?

Perform your new ending for another group. Which ending is more believable and why?

GATHER LANGUAGE

Go through the script one more time and circle phrases and stems that you want to remember for when you have important conversations:

- Dealing with conflict
- Explaining behavior and feelings
- Giving advice/receiving advice
- Telling someone an uncomfortable truth
- Complaining about someone
- Praising/receiving praise

Note: Pay attention to how language used in casual situations is different from more formal situations.

HAVE A MINI-DEBATE

Form two teams and a panel of judges. One team thinks esports are a sport and should be included in competitions among schools. The other team thinks esports is not a sport and should not be recognized by schools. Each team gets a turn to make an argument. Then the other team gets a chance to respond and make a counterargument. You may have three or four rounds of argument and counterargument. The judges can individually write down up to five points for each team at the end of each round. When the debate is over, the judges meet to add their points and declare a winner.

See instructions and materials for structuring a mini-debate on the Alphabet Publishing website at http://www.alphabetpublishingbooks.com/integrated-skills-through-drama.

CREATE A SEQUEL

Work with a partner or in small groups. What do you think Gigi and Oscar's life will be like in the future? Pick a time, such as five or ten years from now and write a short play about their life. You may want to invent new characters.

   a. Three years later, Gigi meets a friend who has opened her own restaurant. They talk about what they are doing and some of the choices they made.
   b. Five years later, Oscar and Gigi are married. They come back to the family home to celebrate a holiday. They share about their lives.

c. Five years later, Oscar has become a famous gamer, but he is now single. He talks to another gamer about the sacrifice he had to make to become a champion.
d. Eight years later, Jaime has finished college with a soccer scholarship. He is offered a chance to join the soccer team in Los Angeles, but his girlfriend has a good job locally. Oscar and Gigi give Jaime advice on what to do.
e. Ten years later. Gigi is happily married to a business person and she has three children. Then she accidentally runs into Oscar at the airport, and they talk about their choices.

PRACTICE PRAGMATICS: MANAGING INTERPERSONAL CONFLICT

a. Read the situations below. What do you say (or do) when someone frustrates or disappoints you?

A person

1. does not come to an appointment or meeting
2. makes a mess and leaves the work for you
3. promises something and then doesn't follow through on the promise
4. takes something without asking
5. forgets something that is important to you

The pragmatics of interpersonal conflict

Even with good intentions, people can sometimes frustrate or disappoint others. When one person expresses frustration, the other person usually tries to repair the situation by explaining their behavior or making an excuse. They might even try to get the other person to laugh or smile. If that doesn't work, the person often moves to making an offer to fix the situation or apologizing.

Note that sometimes people do not say what they mean, so it is important to pay attention to other signals such as indirect language and voice.

You are going to do a role play of an interpersonal conflict.

b. Read the diagram of how a conversation might work.

A is upset by something B has done	*B wants to repair the relationship*
MOVE 1: Raise frustration Greet B and exchange some information. Then introduce your purpose. Express frustration about B's behavior.	
	Respond: Defend yourself with an explanation. Try to get A to understand your reasons.
MOVE 2: Reject B's explanation. Listen to B. Continue to express frustration. Share your feelings and/or the effects of B's behavior.	
	Repair: Listen to A and show you understand. Try to repair the situation. Make an offer to fix the problem or apologize. Try to get the other person to smile.
MOVE 3: Accept repair/apology Listen to B and accept B's offer or apology. Possibly give a warning. Reestablish the relationship, so it ends in a friendly way.	

c. Work in pairs to practice language for dealing with conflict in the table below. Discuss where this language could be used in the conversation diagram on the previous page.

Partner A: Raise frustration	**Partner B: Explain behavior**
The project is due tomorrow, so I'm a little confused. Why haven't you done your part? Is something wrong?	• I tried. I really tried, but . . . • I didn't mean to let you down. It's just that I was . . . • I meant to . . . • I couldn't help it . . . My parents/friends/teacher/girlfriend/boyfriend needed me to . . . • It wasn't my fault. I had to . . . • Yeah, I need to talk to you about that. I was just about to . . . but then . . .
We missed you at dinner the other night. Everyone was expecting you to be there.	
Why were you playing a computer game when you knew you were supposed to pick me up?	

d. Now plan a roleplay by answering the questions below.
- Who are the people having the conversation?
- How well do they know each other?
- How does each person feel?
- Are they equal? Or is one older or of higher status?
- Have you ever experienced a similar situation? What happened?

e. Follow the moves for dealing with interpersonal conflict in the diagram above to create your roleplay.

f. Perform your roleplay for another pair.

g. Watch another pair perform. Then discuss the experience.
- Would you be comfortable with a situation like this in real life?
- Would you use different words or ways of speaking in your first language? Explain.

Additional Practice

a. Close your books and practice the role play without reading your notes. Listen to your partner and try to respond naturally.

b. Choose a new situation. Switch roles and repeat.

Assessment

Choose from the following assessments to reflect and give/get feedback on the experience. You can photocopy the forms in this book or go to http://www.alphabetpublishingbooks.com/integrated-skills-through-drama for downloadable versions.

TEACHER EVALUATION RUBRIC

\multicolumn{4}{c}{Evaluation Rubric for *Only the Best Intentions*}

Actor's name: _____

Check all boxes that apply. Assign one score for each row. Add the two scores for a final score.

	High 50 – 46	*Middle 45–38*	*Low 37–0*
Preparation & Performance /50	☐ has memorized all lines ☐ speaks clearly with appropriate volume ☐ is believable in the role (pragmatics) ☐ responds to other actors realistically	☐ occasionally relies on script or prompting ☐ speaks so audience can hear ☐ is mostly believable in the role (pragmatics) ☐ attends to other actors naturally most of the time	☐ uses script ☐ speaks quietly or quickly so it is difficult to understand ☐ is not believable or breaks character, e.g., by laughing ☐ unnatural, inattentive, or unemotional response to other actors
	High 50–46	**Middle 45–38**	**Low 37–0**
Language Delivery /50	☐ conveys emotions through intonation and gesture ☐ uses effective sentence and word stress ☐ has clear pronunciation	☐ uses some intonation and gesture ☐ uses sentence and word stress most of the time ☐ has comprehensible pronunciation	☐ lack of intonation and gesture weaken emotional message ☐ errors with sentence and word stress make comprehension difficult ☐ has pronunciation issues that interfere with comprehensibility
Total /100			

PEER FEEDBACK QUESTIONS

1. Ask another actor questions to learn more about their performance.

    a. What were your goals in creating your character and preparing for the performance?

    b. What did you enjoy about the process?

    c. What was hardest for you?

    d. Did you develop any skills? Explain.

2. Tell the actor about your experience watching the play. You may use the stems below or your own ideas.

    a. I think your character was . . .

    b. My favorite part was when . . .

    c. I'd like to know more about . . .

SELF-REFLECTION QUESTIONS

Actor's name: _____

Write three or four sentences explaining your answers to the questions below.

1. How did you prepare for your role?

2. Did anything happen that surprised you?

3. Did your language and/or conversation skills improve?

4. How do you feel about the performance?

5. What advice would you give to other actors?

Beyond the Classroom

PUBLISH AN INTERVIEW ABOUT SCREEN TIME

Do Some Research.

Choose one of the following activities:

- ☐ **Interview** someone about his or her screen activities. Consider the following questions and/or write your own.

  - How much time do you spend on a screen each day?
  - What do you do on your screen(s) for work, socializing, or fun?
  - How do screens make your life better?
  - Is there anything you would like to change about your screen habits?
  - How does your family feel about your use of screens?
  - Would you say screens are an important part of your social life?

- ☐ **Use the Internet** to find a video of someone talking about screens, gaming, or other online activities in English. Be sure to put the link to the video on your paper. Watch the video and take notes.

Write a Draft

Reread the article *Family Life in the Age of Screens* on page 69. Can you make any connections between your notes and the ideas in the article? Then write your draft. You might find it helpful to discuss the answer to one interview question in each paragraph. Also try to use direct quotes. They will make your paper more interesting.

Alternatively, you could record your interview and create a podcast. If you do this, make sure you have a clear recording without background noise so listeners can understand. You can also give your own opinions about the interview and include them into your final product.

Get Feedback

Exchange papers with a partner, and read your partner's paper. You may not feel comfortable with editing, but you can tell your partner where you are confused. Also tell your partner about the parts you enjoy or want to learn more about.

If you are doing a podcast, you can give your partner feedback on the recording.

Revise

Read your paper and make improvements. Some writers find they say something twice in different words, so they need to cut unnecessary details. Other writers find they want to add new details when they revise. When you finish, your paragraphs should all be similar in size, and your sentences should not be too long. A combination of short and long sentences is usually effective.

If you are doing a podcast, listen and revise any parts that are unclear.

Present.

Give a talk about your investigation into screen time in groups or to the whole class so people can learn about different careers. Ask and answer questions. Then turn in your product for a grade.

Edit

Edit your paper for mistakes and punctuation. Make final changes. Then turn in your final draft.

Sample Performance Daily Schedule

Goal	Time	Activity
Warm-up	10 minutes	Cast assembles and sets up the stage.
Introduce Theme Critical thinking question	10 – 15 minutes	The director introduces a discussion topic, the critical thinking question of the play. The director invites students to do a pair-share about the following question. *How should you prepare for family life in the age of screens?*
Prepare audience	1 minute	Director introduces the play and asks people to turn off their cell phones.
Performance	20 minutes	Cast performs the play and takes a curtain call.
Post-Play Talkback	10 – 15 minutes	Director passes out paper for small groups to prepare questions for talkback. Director facilitates the talkback in which audience makes comments or asks the actors questions.

About the Author

ALICE SAVAGE comes from a family of theatre people. Her grandfather was a professor of theatre arts, and her father is a playwright. This drama background combined with a love of teaching has given her the opportunity to bring two passions together. In addition to *Only the Best Intentions*, Savage has also written *Her Own Worst Enemy* and *Rising Water* for Alphabet Press.

Currently, a professor of ESOL at Lone Star College System, in Houston, Texas, she is grateful for the opportunity to spend time with young people who are figuring out their own relationships with screens and humans.

www.ingramcontent.com/pod-product-compliance
Lightning Source LLC
LaVergne TN
LVHW080303260326
834688LV00043B/1230